From A Soldier Of Rome To A Soldier For Christ

An Easter Sunrise Drama

Lawrence H. Balleine

CSS Publishing Company, Inc., Lima, Ohio

FROM A SOLDIER OF ROME TO A SOLDIER FOR CHRIST

For more information about CSS Publishing Company resources, visit our website at www.csspub.com or email us at custserv@csspub.com or call (800) 241-4056.

Cover design by Barbara Spencer
ISBN 0-7880-2392-6

PRINTED IN U.S.A.

*Dedicated to
the confirmation class
of Zwingli United Church of Christ
of Monticello, Wisconsin,
who presented this Easter drama
for the first time*

From A Soldier Of Rome To A Soldier For Christ

Cast (in order of appearance)
Narrator
Roman Soldier
Jesus
Crowd Of Followers (four to six)
Faithful Women (two)
Angry Crowd (Crowd Of Followers)
Two Pharisees
Pontius Pilate
Servant Of Pilate
Joseph Of Arimathea
Angel
Stage Crew

Props

Two chairs — one for Pontius Pilate and one for Narrator
Large cross (8' to 9' in height)
Two matching votive candles in clear glass containers
Hammer and three large spikes
One 2" x 4" approximately 1' in length
One white handkerchief (burial cloth)
Bowl filled with water
Towel
Papier-mâché stone (2' to 3' in diameter)
Card table covered with black cloth
Altar candles
White altar cloth, lectern and pulpit covers
Easter banners
Easter flowers

Costumes

Narrator — modern "dress" clothing

Roman Soldier — appropriate military dress (sword and helmet are optional)

Jesus — white robe

Crowd Of Followers — simple peasant clothing

Faithful Women — simple peasant clothing

Pharisees — more elaborate and stunning than Followers

Pontius Pilate — elaborate robe

Servant Of Pilate — peasant clothing

Joseph Of Arimathea — somewhat more elaborate clothing than crowd

Angel — white robe (halo and wings are optional)

Set Specifications

(See sketch on page 7) Narrator speaks from pulpit. A chair is located immediately behind the pulpit. A chair is placed centrally on the chancel level. A large cross is placed stage right on the nave level. A card table covered with black cloth and a large stone is placed on the nave level to the immediate left or right of the chancel steps. Right and left entrance/exits on both chancel and nave levels would be helpful.

Set Specifications

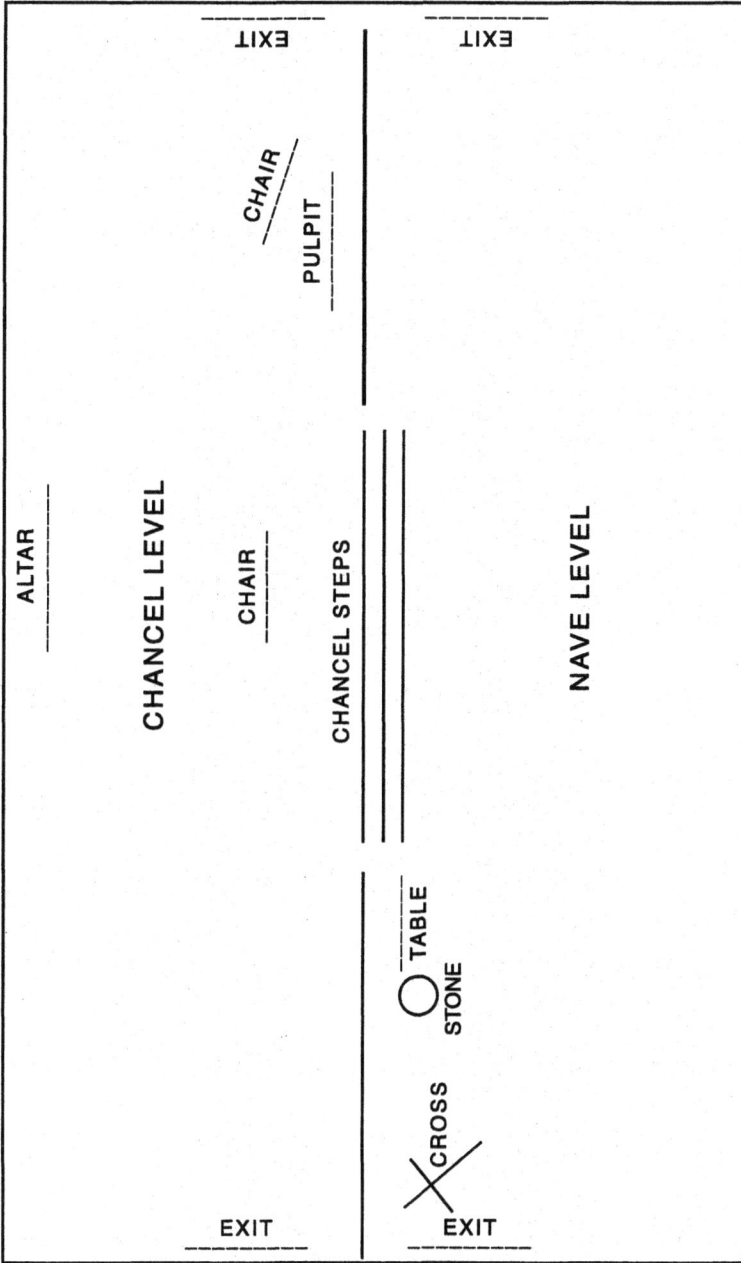

EXIT

EXIT

CHAIR

PULPIT

ALTAR

CHANCEL LEVEL

CHAIR

CHANCEL STEPS

NAVE LEVEL

TABLE

STONE

CROSS

EXIT

EXIT

From A Soldier Of Rome
To A Soldier For Christ

(Narrator enters upper stage left and stands at pulpit or lectern.)

Introduction

Narrator: I appreciate the opportunity to speak with you this morning. I am Maximus Minimus, a former Roman soldier who served in the Palestine province. I grew up near Rome and was glad to serve my emperor. When I was given the opportunity to travel with the army I was eager to engage in this venture. I was sent to the province of Palestine, located on the eastern shore of the Mediterranean. There I was assigned to Pontius Pilate, the governor of the province.

Scene 1

(Roman Soldier, Jesus, Crowd Of Followers, Faithful Women, and Two Pharisees enter lower stage left.)

Narrator: *(speaking from pulpit or lectern)* My first post was in the Galilean countryside. That's me over there *(points to Roman Soldier)*. I was assigned to watch the crowds who had gathered to see and hear an itinerant preacher and teacher whose name was Jesus of Nazareth.

This Jesus had a remarkable message. It was one of love and peace. Being a Roman soldier, that was a rather strange message for me to hear. All I heard about were stories of war and rumors of war.

As the crowds flocked to see and hear him I, too, found myself drawn in by what he had to say: "Blessed are the peacemakers, for they will be called children of God." "Do not store up treasures on earth, but store up for yourselves treasures in heaven; for where your treasure is, there your heart will be also." "Do not judge one another. For with the judgment you make, you will be judged, and the measure you give will be the measure you get." "If anyone strikes you on the right cheek, turn the other, also. And if anyone wants to sue you and take your coat, give him your cloak as well." "Love your enemies; pray for those who persecute you."

Yes, this man Jesus had an amazing message; and he taught with a kind of authority quite different from anything I had ever experienced. *(takes seat behind pulpit)*

(Exit lower stage left: Jesus, Faithful Women, Two Pharisees, Roman Soldier. Roman Soldier prepares to enter upper stage right.)

Congregation sings "Teach Me, O Lord, Thy Holy Way."

Scene 2
(Pontius Pilate enters upper stage right and sits on chair.)

Narrator: *(stands and speaks from pulpit)* The Jewish festival of Passover neared, and with large crowds expected in Jerusalem — the Holy City of the Jews — I was reassigned to the city. I was given a position as one of the soldiers in the governor's palace. Palatial duties. "I've got it 'made in the shade,' " I thought. What an honor it was to serve Pontius Pilate in his court.

(Jesus enters lower stage left being escorted by Two Pharisees and Angry Crowd.)

Narrator: Early one Friday morning I was awakened and called to my post. A mob of folks led by two Jewish leaders had brought a prisoner to Pontius Pilate's court, and they wanted Pilate to sentence him. They wanted the man executed. When I went to my post in the courtyard, I could hardly believe my eyes.

(Roman Soldier enters upper stage right and stands to the right of Pilate.)

10

Narrator: The prisoner was Jesus of Nazareth whom I had seen many times in the Galilean countryside. So many people appeared to love him then. I wondered what had happened. How could such love and admiration turn to such hate?

I learned later that many wanted him to be a king and to overthrow our government, but when he did not advocate such violence, his own people turned against him. They brought false accusations against him, and Pilate kept telling the crowd: "I find no fault in this man." Finally, just to satisfy the crowd, Pilate ordered Jesus to be whipped. He thought this would appease the mob.

(Roman Soldier steps down and escorts Jesus. They exit lower stage right. After they exit, a whipping sound is made — offstage.)

Narrator: I have had to do some awful things in my life as a soldier of Rome, but this was one of the most distasteful things I've ever had to do. Other soldiers made fun of Jesus; some hit him with a stick. Yet others put a purple robe on him and danced around him and said: "Hail, King of the Jews," because the soldiers had heard people refer to him as "the king of the Jews." *(takes seat behind pulpit)*

Congregation sings "Ah, Holy Jesus" verses 1 and 2.

Scene 3

Narrator: *(stands and speaks from pulpit)* After Jesus was whipped, Pilate had us march Jesus back into the courtyard. Pilate assumed the crowd would now be satisfied.

(Jesus and Roman Soldier enter lower stage right and take their places before Pilate.)

Narrator: Pilate, knowing the rumor about Jesus being considered a king, said in jest: "Behold your king." But the blood-thirsty crowd still wasn't satisfied. To his surprise the crowd yelled back:

11

Angry Crowd: We have no king but Caesar!

Narrator: "Then what should I do with Jesus?" asks Pilate.

Angry Crowd: *(yells)* Crucify him! Crucify him!

Narrator: Then Pilate suggested that he could grant amnesty to a prisoner. Barabbas was being held for committing murder in a revolt. Pilate — thinking the crowd would choose to have Jesus released instead of this notorious Barabbas — suggested: "Shall I release Barabbas or this Jesus?" And the crowd shouted:

Angry Crowd: *(shouts)* Barabbas! Give us Barabbas!

Narrator: "Then what should I do with Jesus?" asks Pilate.

Angry Crowd: *(yells)* Crucify him! Crucify him!

Narrator: And then the crowd said something that really alarmed Pilate. I could see it in his eyes. They shouted: "You are not a friend of Caesar if you release Jesus of Nazareth." Pilate feared Caesar more than anyone else. Caesar — the one who had appointed Pilate to his position as governor. Pilate knew Caesar held his destiny. If Pontius Pilate lost Caesar's favor, he might find himself out of a job; he might even be demoted.

Calling for a bowl, Pilate washed his hands and said to the crowd: "The blood of this man is not on my hands, but on yours."

(Servant Of Pilate enters upper stage right carrying a bowl; Pilate washes his hands and Servant exits upper stage right.)

Narrator: Then Pilate gave the order that Jesus was to be crucified.

(Jesus is led away by the Roman Soldier with the crowd following — exit lower stage left.)

Congregation sings "Were You There," verse 1.

Scene 4

(Roman Soldier enters lower stage left and carries a lighted candle across front of stage and kneels at the base of the cross. Faithful Women follow Soldier and kneel at the base of the cross. Roman Soldier pounds spikes into a 2" x 4", then carries the lighted candle up to the cross and places it on a small platform located at the cross-section of the cross. Roman Soldier descends the ladder and stands off to the immediate right side of the cross and gazes upon it.)

Narrator: I was given the order to carry out the execution. I led Jesus out to Golgotha where the crucifixion was to take place. Then I pounded the nails into Jesus' hands. It is then that I looked into his eyes. They were not filled with hate or contempt, but with compassion.

What was I doing, carrying out the execution of this innocent man? Then I thought: I am just fulfilling my duties as a Roman soldier. It is my job. It is not my fault. I did not order this done.

While on the cross, when Jesus said: "Father, forgive them for they do not know what they are doing," I felt he was speaking directly to me. Here he was on the cross — dying — and he is pleading with his God to have mercy on his accusers, and also — I felt — on me.

(Darken room and pause)

Narrator: After being on the cross a few hours, darkness covered the earth for what seemed to be an eternity. The earth shook and Jesus cried out with a loud voice: "It is finished!" And then he died.

(Roman Soldier climbs the ladder and extinguishes the candle; then descends the ladder and stands at the front of the cross facing the extinguished candle.)

13

Narrator: At that very instant I knew — I knew there was something special about this man, and for some unknown reason I blurted out: "Surely this man is the Son of God."

How could I say such a thing? I had never before believed in anything but the power of Rome. I hoped word would not get around as to what I had said. I could be in serious trouble.

Congregation sings "My Faith Looks Up To Thee."

(After verse 3, Roman Soldier exits lower stage right and Faithful Women exit slowly lower stage left, then proceed [unseen by audience] to the rear of the sanctuary and wait to re-enter sanctuary in a later scene.)

Scene 5
(Pontius Pilate enters upper stage right on verse 4 of "My Faith Looks Up To Thee" and sits on throne. After Pilate is seated, Roman Soldier and Joseph Of Arimathea enter upper stage right and stand before Pilate.)

Narrator: Later that day, one whom I imagined to be a follower of Jesus came asking for the body of Jesus. Pilate asked me if Jesus was dead. When I reported that he was, Pilate gave this man permission to take the body of Jesus for burial.

(Joseph Of Arimathea moves to the cross and climbs up the ladder and wraps Jesus' body [the candle] in a handkerchief and places it in the grave [card table] and rolls the stone in front of the candle.)

Congregation sings "Were You There?" verse 5.

Scene 6
(Two Pharisees enter lower stage left and stand in front of Pontius Pilate. Roman Soldier continues to stand to the right of Pilate.)

Narrator: Then Pilate got a strange request. Some of the leaders of the Jews approached Pilate and reported what Jesus said while he was still alive: "After three days I will rise again." So they asked Pilate that the tomb be made secure until the third day. They said: "Otherwise his disciples may go and steal him away and tell the people, 'He has been raised from the dead.'"

Then Pontius Pilate gave the order for a guard to be placed at the tomb. I volunteered for this guard duty. That's the least I could do for this man, Jesus, whom I had come to appreciate and admire. I could protect his grave so no robber could desecrate his burial place.

(Two Pharisees exit lower stage left. Roman Soldier takes his place just to the right of the tomb and Pilate exits upper stage right.)

Narrator: Sometime during Saturday night — it was late in the night — possibly even on toward morning — toward dawn — the earth shook and a great light shone forth and I was overcome. I seemed to be knocked unconscious.

(Chancel lights are quickly and repeatedly flashed off and on. Roman Soldier appears overcome. Angel enters lower stage left, rolls away stone [continuing to hide the candle behind the stone] and sits alongside the tomb.)

Narrator: When I awakened I could hardly believe my eyes. The stone, which had been rolled in front of the grave, had now been rolled away, and I could not see the body of Jesus in the grave.

I had failed in my duty. I was afraid for my life. I decided to hide nearby.

(Roman Soldier hides lower stage left.)

Narrator: Soon, within minutes, I saw two women — followers of Jesus — coming to the tomb.

(Faithful Women enter from the back of the sanctuary and proceed to the tomb.)

Narrator: When the women looked inside the tomb, they did not see the body of Jesus. Then I noticed what appeared to be an angel, and this angel spoke to the women saying: "Why do you look for the living among the dead? He is not here, but he has risen. Remember how he told you while he was still in Galilee that the Son of Man must be handed over to sinners, be crucified, and on the third day rise again"? Then the women remembered Jesus' words, and they left the tomb.

(Faithful Women exit and proceed to the back of the sanctuary. Roman Soldier exits lower stage left.)

Narrator: The women return to the disciples and announce:

Faithful Women: *(speaking from the back of the sanctuary)* He is risen!

(Narrator takes seat behind pulpit.)

Congregation sings "Christ The Lord Is Risen Today."

(During the introductory notes of the hymn, Angel exits lower stage left; and the Faithful Women re-enter from the back of the sanctuary carrying a lighted candle matching the one that had been placed in the tomb. This re-lighted candle is placed on the altar and Faithful Women light the altar candles from the light of the candle. As the Congregation sings "Christ The Lord Is Risen Today" all sanctuary lights are turned on. The sanctuary is transformed as a white altar cloth, and white lectern and pulpit coverings are put in place, Easter banners are hung, and all Easter flowers are brought in and placed appropriately in the chancel. These tasks are done by the stage crew.)

Scene 7

Roman Soldier: *(enters from upper stage left and speaks from pulpit)* I must find the followers of Jesus, and I must tell them. I no longer wish to be a soldier of Rome. I want to be a soldier for this Jesus whom you call the Christ. I was a soldier of Rome. Now I am a soldier for Jesus Christ.

Congregation sings "Soldiers Of Christ, Arise."